MW00425576

ENTER THE NAVEL

For the Love of Creative Nonfiction

Anjoli Roy

THE OPERATING SYSTEM DIGITAL PRINT//DOCUMENT

ENTER THE NAVEL:
FOR THE LOVE OF CREATIVE NONFICTION

ISBN # 978-1-946031-60-0
copyright © 2020 by Anjoli Roy
edited and designed by ELÆ [Lynne DeSilva-Johnson] and Orchid Tierney

For additional questions regarding reproduction, quotation, or to request a pdf for review contact operator@theoperatingsystem.org

Print books from The Operating System are distributed to the trade by SPD/Small Press Distribution, with ePub and POD via Ingram, with production by Spencer Printing, in Honesdale, PA, in the USA. Digital books are available directly from the OS, direct from authors, via DIY pamplet printing, and/or POD.

This text was set in Arial, Europa, Minion, and OCR-A Standard.
Spiral svg: https://pixabay.com/vectors/spiral-swirl-white-design-305142/

Cover Art by ELÆ [Lynne DeSilva-Johnson]

[Cover Image Description: Title in white, author's name in black, superimposed on aquatic biota in pink. Back Cover Description: "Bloom. Mutation. Entropy. Catalyst. Brine." in white. Publisher and copyright in black.]

the operating system
www.theoperatingsystem.org
mailto: operator@theoperatingsystem.org

ENTER THE NAVEL
For the Love of Creative Nonfiction

2020 OS SYSTEM OPERATORS

CREATIVE DIRECTOR/FOUNDER/MANAGING EDITOR: ELÆ
[Lynne DeSilva-Johnson]

DIGITAL CHAPBOOKS: Curtis Emery, Orchid Tierney

The Operating System is a member of the Radical Open Access Collective, a community of scholar-led, not-for-profit presses, journals and other open access projects. Now consisting of 40 members, we promote a progressive vision for open publishing in the humanities and social sciences.

Learn more at: http://radicaloa.disruptivemedia.org.uk/about/

Your donation makes our publications, platform and programs possible! We <3 You. http://www.theoperatingsystem.org/subscribe-join/

TABLE OF CONTENTS

Abdomen	8
Bacteria	9
Center	10
Depression	11
Emit	12
First	13
Geography	14
Horse	16
Innies	17
Junction	18
Kangaroo	19
Lint	20
Mother	21
Navel-Gazer	25
Orange	26
Piercing	27
Question	29
Regret	30
Sexy	31
Television	32
Umbilicus	33
Vishnu	34
Wheel	37
Xenial	38
Yolk stalk	39
Zzzzzz	40
About the Author	53

ABDOMEN

It's common knowledge that the navel is a round scar in the middle of a person's abdomen produced from the severing of the umbilical cord. An equivalent mark exists on most other mammals, since the mammalian fetus obtains oxygen and nutrients through their abdomen from their birthing mother through the blood vessels of the umbilical cord.

Dolphins have navels.

Platypuses do not.

Today, the navel is a gate surgeons pass through to enter the body. Via a small incision, they can now remove whole organs. Over the telephone and while eating dinner, gynecologists like my dad have directed nervous interns to conduct laparoscopic hysterectomies without creating a new scar.

"No, no! That's the bladder! Move that to the side!" he once said, sucking dal from his fingers.

We were sitting around the table. My first sleepover friend from my mostly white elementary school sat frozen at the table beside me, stunned already by the challenge of eating Indian food, let alone eating it with her hands. I eventually got up to get her a spoon.[1]

The navel might just be a scar. It might be the threshold to the spiritual realm—to our ancestors and those not yet born. It might be something else.

---

1. See "What Babas Are For" for a more complete telling of this story.

In 2012, a team of ecologists in North Carolina published a scientific research paper on their Belly Button Biodiversity project study.[2] They collected samples from sixty people's navels and found 2,300 different types of bacteria living in those human belly buttons.

The unique combination of a person's navel bacteria varies from person to person.

A person's belly button was found with a bacterium previously discovered only in soil samples from Japan. This person had never visited Japan.

Another bacterium found in a sample from one person's navel had previously only been found in the ocean.

One individual who reported not to have showered or bathed for several years presented with extremophile bacteria—that is, bacteria known to live under extreme environmental conditions, such as ice caps and thermal vents.[3]

What are we to do with this information? I ask because there are disgusting things like cheese made from human navel bacteria,[4] and I'm not sure what to do with that.

Go ahead.

Look it up.

Shudder if you need to, as I did.

---

2. See Hulcr, et al.
3. See Fischer.
4. See Kim and Jones.

CENTER

The navel

is the middle   point of anything—

the hub   or heart of an

organization,   or the middle of

a sphere of activity.

Maya, who is the middle of our parents' three daughters, said that when she'd play basketball one-on-one with our dad, he would watch her navel closely to anticipate her next move, blocking her efforts to make a basket.

"It was maddening. It also made me laugh," she said.

In this story, our dad was a literal navel-gazer, a term we'll come to (see Navel-Gazer).

In conchology, or the study of mollusk shells, the central depression formed by the inner whorls of a gastropod shell is called a navel.[5]

Post-partum depression affects 10 to 20 percent of humans who give birth every year.[6] To stave off this depression, some ingest their own placentas dried and encapsulated, or cooked, or raw in smoothies.

My oldest sister, Joya, birthed seven children and says that ingesting encapsulated placenta helped her counteract the huge drop in progesterone after birth, which can trigger, in its mildest form, the baby blues.

"It felt like a grandma stroking my hair, encouraging and gentle and subtle . . . like a presence was there," she said.

She would take the placenta pills when she was feeling tender or overwhelmed.

The placenta is the organ that connects, via the umbilical cord, to the belly of the fetus, where the navel is made after birth.

---

5. If you are someone fascinated by mollusks in general and abalone in particular, you might like to read my "Grandpa Was a Skin Diver," which is forthcoming with *Anomaly* as of this writing. (You and I might be alone in this curiosity.)
6. See Illinois Department of Public Health.

EMIT

Some of us have deeper navels than others (see Innies).

Based on the accumulation of bacteria and physical objects (see Lint), those with deeper navels are probably at a higher risk of emitting navel odor.

While, in general, our skin hosts a variety of bacteria crucial to the strength of our body's immune system, some bacteria, when entering or residing long enough in the navel, start to do strange things.

Staphylococcus epidermis, when living in the belly button, where oxygen is in short supply, ferments sugars and creates what has been called "a teeny tiny bit of navel wine."[7]

Though I do not have omphalophobia—or a fear of navels that can trigger disgust or terror even from glimpsing a belly button, a fear that can be triggered from seeing one's own navel too—I do not like other people to touch my belly button. I'm not sure if it's the "navel wine" mentioned above that's doing it, but I do know from personal experience that belly button smell can range from mild to rank.

I may or may not have pushed away wandering hands from my navel for this reason.

---

7. See The Public Science Lab, "Common Belly Button Bacteria."

The navel is our first wound.

GEOGRAPHY

The navel is the center or middle point of a country or sea.

In the town of Shibukawa, located in the center of Japan, an annual festival celebrates the belly button. Shibukawa is called the belly button of Japan.[8]

In Hinduism, one navel is a geographic marker so crucial, it is considered to be the source of the universe (see Vishnu).

A mountain can also be a navel. Located on the largest of the Hawaiian islands, Maunakea is the tallest mountain in the world measured from the sea floor. Kānaka Maoli, the Indigenous of Hawai'i, recognize Maunakea as a piko.[9]

A piko is a summit or top of a hill or a mountain. A piko is also a navel, navel string, or umbilical cord. It is the place where leaf attaches to stem.

Maunakea is piko, is earth, is land, is 'āina, or that which feeds. For Kānaka Maoli, 'āina is more than geography. 'Āina is ancestor. 'Āina is sacred.

#protectmaunakea
#KūKia'iMauna

Maunakea is a mountain child of Wākea (Sky Father) and Papa (Earth Mother). The peak of the mountain is the piko of the island child, the place where land connects to sky.

From these divine parents, a human named Hāloa, a name that means long stalk, was born. Before Hāloa came a stillborn. This first child was planted in the ground and, in turn, became the first kalo plant, whose heart-shaped leaves emerged from long stems.

Hāloa has the responsibility of caring for his older brother, the kalo plant. In turn, the kalo plant cares for Hāloa as his important food and ancestor.

Kanaka Maoli families rooted to Maunakea have placed the umbilical cords of newborn children on Maunakea. In this way, human navels connect to mountain navel.

Upholding and turning to Indigenous relationships to land that care for and protect that which cares for and protects you, as in Hāloa's relationship with kalo, is likely central to our survival as a species in this climate-change-addled anthropocene.

As Kanaka Maoli scholar Bryan Kamaoli Kuwada has said famously, "We live in the future. Come join us."

---

8. See Muramoto.
9. This discussion of Maunakea and the retelling of the story of Hāloa come from discussions with Dr. Bryan Kamaoli Kuwada and references to Kepa Maly and Onaona Maly and *Nā Puke Wehewehe ʻŌlelo Hawaiʻi*'s entry on "piko."

HORSE

A navel has been a name for the middle point of a horse's back. This definition is obsolete.

Thirty-year-old University of Arkansas student Randon Beasley, on August 31, 2010, made the world record for most quarters fit inside a navel. His is so deep, he fit 30 coins inside and, as the world criteria requires, stood for the duration of his attempt, with all quarters remaining in the belly button unassisted for at least 3 seconds.

Related records indicate that the most blueberries fit into a belly button are 10.[10]

I could not find information on record-setting outies, though if you look around long enough, you will likely come across a story about a 26-year-old who had a navel that stuck out a full inch from his belly and was offered upward of $1,000 dollars by fetishists for a video of him fondling it.[11]

You might shudder at that too, as I did.

It's kind of a mystery why some folks have innies and some folks have outies, particularly since the way the navel forms doesn't—contrary to some public opinion—depend on how the umbilical cord is cut.

Even innies come in their own shapes. Some innies heal in the shape of a spiral, like the new navel of my sister Maya's just-born baby, Rey.

Only 10 percent of people have outies in adulthood. Innies are perceived as being more attractive.[12]

In 2018, *Allure* magazine reported that umbilicoplasty, or plastic surgery to "fix" the belly button, was trending.[13]

Many want to change an outie to an innie.

Tummy tucks sometimes involve the "beautifying" of the navel.

---

10. See Henderson and Rollman.
11. See UNILAD.
12. See American Museum of Natural History.
13. See MacKenzie.

JUNCTION

In English, a navel is also defined as the junction of leaf and stem. This definition is obsolete, though it remains intact in Hawaiian.

I wonder if this linguistic severing of Anglophone navels, of the cutting of kinship of plant navels from human navels, might not illustrate how and why so many human communities live like lands and waters are endless commodities to consume, develop, and pollute rather than care for, are beings that we have dominion over and therefore the right to abuse.

As stated earlier, I wonder if mending this wound— and putting our weight behind those communities with enduring, reciprocal navel connections—might be key to the survival of the human species (see Geography).

KANGAROO

The kangaroo is another mammal without a navel.

LINT

The lint in human navels is mostly made up of clothing fibers, hair, and dead skin cells.

Lint collecting is an actual hobby. The artist Rachel Betty Case has made from belly button lint tiny smiling bears that she traps in bottles.[14]

In 2010, the Guinness Book of Records recognized librarian Graham Barker for his collection of belly button lint. Over the course of 26 years, the 45-year-old collected 22.1 grams of the stuff, which would be the equivalent of 110 carats if the lint were actually precious stones or pearls. He sold three jars of his lint to a museum, presumably for display.

I'm curious which museum would bother to buy that. I'm also curious how much he sold it for.

Barker has been quoted as saying, "I will stop collecting when I'm no longer physically capable."[15]

I wonder if he's still at it.

14. See Sabrina.
15. See Daily Mail Reporter.

The navel is the mark that ties us to the person who gives birth to us.

My white momma doesn't have a belly button. Or, rather, she doesn't have the one she was born with. It was removed when she had a tummy tuck in the early 90s, when I, her youngest, was about seven years old.

The tummy tuck was an afterthought, actually, because she'd decided to have a voluntary hysterectomy after receiving an abnormal result from a precancerous pap smear. Her aunt Anna was in the late stages of ovarian cancer, and our mom didn't want to take chances with the possibility of getting sick. She and our brown dad were also divorcing. Her health coverage was running out. She was going back to school full time too, and she knew that frequent doctor visits to keep an eye on her cervix weren't going to be feasible, financially or time wise. She'd already stopped menstruating, so it didn't seem like the hysterectomy would be a big deal.

Since they were going to do an abdominal approach for the total hysterectomy—laparoscopic hysterectomies hadn't been developed yet—she asked if they would get someone in there to tighten things up a little before they sewed her close.

"Two for the price of one, right?" she said.

The incision would be way down by her pelvic bone. The doctors would free up her skin on her abdomen, including her belly button, and pull it down and then poke a hole again where the belly button was.

It would have looked weird *not* to have a belly button, she said.

To create her new navel, the doctors sutured around the tissue and then packed it down to the residual scar of her umbilical cord.

"It made a nasty looking thing," she said. "I look at that sucker and I think, well, fuck that."

She accepted, sadly, that she would never again wear a

skimpy two-piece bathing suit.[16]

The combined hysterectomy and tummy tuck (and new navel) had more of an impact than she'd anticipated. She mentioned a woman she met who hadn't had a normal bowel movement for nine years after her hysterectomy.

"*Nine years,*" she said. "That depressed me so bad."

I asked her how that could happen.

She talked about the adhesions that form, sticking things together that aren't supposed to be stuck together. "I have an adhesion and I know exactly where that sucker is, on the lower right abdomen."

She ended up in the hospital once because her intestine got caught around the adhesion and pinched. It was really miserable.

I imagined her small intestine, slithering around during digestion, always threatening to get snagged.

I asked her if she missed her old navel.

"It was a lot prettier before I had this done. I probably would have been just as happy without one. I could've seen if the guys were paying attention." She said this laughing.

In the mid-90s, around the time that Joan Osborne dropped the famous song "What If God Was One of Us," a tip circulated in my sixth-grade friend group at our Christian elementary school about belly buttons and God: If someone claimed that they were God, we'd know they were telling the truth if they didn't have a belly button. God surely never would have been born in a human way: with moms and placentas and umbilical-cord-severing that would result in a scar. This story made sense to us, even though the story of Jesus's human birth had been drilled into our heads.

Despite my agnosticism, it took me years to untangle the accidental subversion of this theory despite our Christian training.

I wonder if, when I was in the sixth grade, my mom no

longer had a navel, I would have looked at her differently.

The alphabet doesn't have a navel. Since it has 26 letters, and 26 is an even number, there is no middle letter. Or, we might say that the space between the M and the N is the invisible navel. In this essay, that navel would be right here.

---

16. Although it's difficult to admit, I am indebted to my mother's previous ability to wear skimpy two-pieces. My parents first flirted at a pool, where my mom wore a tiny two-piece. As she sauntered by on her way up to her room, she tossed her magazine to the man she noticed was checking her out. The lead headline on the magazine was something like "Everything You Wanted to Know about Sex but Were Too Afraid to Ask." Parents are so disgusting. (See "Little Red BMW" for a fuller retelling of this story.)

NAVEL-GAZER

Navel-gazer is an insult usually launched at someone who is self-absorbed, who positions their own thoughts and ideas at the expense of a wider view, as if such things are interesting or insightful for anyone other than themselves.

Belly button meditation is a real thing, though. Contemplation of one's navel, or omphaloskepsis, comes from the ancient Greek, and involves the use of the navel as an aid in the quest to consider the cosmos or human nature or to converse with the divine. Some say they have experienced celestial joy during navel-gazing.

There are actual marble statues depicting omphaloskepsis. In the Louvre, four Roman men stand hunched over awkwardly, regarding their alabaster abs.[17]

"Their *abs. Right*," my mom said when I told her this. "You sure they weren't 'questing' for something a little lower?"

In yoga, the navel is an important chakra in the body. Named manipura, or "city of jewels," this chakra is supposed to provide a practitioner of yoga with a clear sense of self and purpose,[18] though it's unclear whether, in all the different kinds of yoga that exist today, the physical act of bending one's upper back to look at one's navel has been utilized to engage this chakra.

I am not a practitioner of yoga, and therefore cannot speak to that.

---

17. See *Satyres In Atlante*.
18. See "Manipura Chakra."

ORANGE

A navel is a kind of orange. It is also the name of the small secondary fruit at the apex of a navel orange: the orange inside the orange.

My mom's parents were smart about oranges. They had navel and Valencia trees, which fruit at different times during the year. This meant fresh oranges year round.

Grandma would squeeze these fruits into juice that she'd serve in shot-size glasses to her wee granddaughters. Even now, decades since my last glass, Grandma's fresh-squeezed juice is the best I've had.

When we were little, my sisters and I learned to sip it slowly.

I remember learning in reproductive biology that female babies are born with all the eggs they'll ever have in their lives. I learned that this biological reality is completely unlike males, who make and dispense of 1,500 sperm per second.

In this sense, females are like nested dolls: to carry a female fetus is to carry all your potential grandchildren too.

The belief that we are born with all the eggs we'll ever have has been challenged,[19] but I like this idea that I may have been, on some cellular level, drinking my grandmother's orange juice while my grandma was pregnant with my mother, who was already carrying in her body many of the basic building blocks of potential me.

I like this idea of fetus navels connected to invisible maternal navels, backward and forward for eternity.

---

19. See Dell'Amore.

On average, it takes six to twelve months to heal from belly button piercing.

Even though I hate to have my belly button touched, I got mine pierced.

I was sixteen and, along with my girlfriends, had decided to, maybe ironically, maybe unironically, pull the stunt of telling each of our parents that we were sleeping over at the other's house so we could stay out all night. The six or so of us slid across the sheep-skinned seats of my dad's two-door 1972 cherry red Mercedes to head to Venice Beach so Briana could get her belly button pierced. But, by the time we got there, she looked like she was going to chicken out.

To be fair, the sun was kissing the ocean once we finally made it to the Westside and found parking and had clamored onto the boardwalk. Hardly anyone was in sight. No rollerbladers. No swole folks at Muscle Beach. The street vendors were packing up henna stands and live-art supplies. The scene was just missing a cartoon tumbleweed.

We hustled to the piercing studio we'd visited in weekends past and caught a guy just as he was pulling down the metal security gate. He doubted our age. We showed him some cash. He let us in.

"I don't know . . ." Briana said once we were inside, where the needles were.

"I'll do it!" I said.

Were we rebelling by piercing our belly buttons? Were we taking back our first connection? (See Mother.)

I remember the tiny room he led us to. The surgical gloves and the bite of an alcohol swab on warm teenage skin. It hurt more than I thought was necessary.

"He did it deep," Briana would later tell me warily. I didn't know because I couldn't bear to watch him.

In retrospect, it was pretty clear that guy wasn't a piercer, but in this moment, swept up as we were in the

Dawson's Creek, *Empire Records*, Mariah Carey-at-her-peak swoon of our high school years, there was no backing down. Teenage slogan: no regrets.

Briana followed through too. And so we became piercing twins during what would become the gruesome healing.

"Is it supposed to be like this?" she asked.

I had no idea.

The morning after, when she tried to move the stud, as we were instructed to do, Briana passed out.

"I had this huge bruise on my ear from falling in the shower," she said.

We filled actual shot glasses with hydrogen peroxide, which we suctioned onto our bleeding navels for a cleaning bath. We rotated the studs to keep the ever-present crust at bay. We spent a lot of time with our backs bent, contemplating our navels, just as we simultaneously tried to ignore the oozing. But this was not omphaloskepsis.

All in all, it took close to a year of grossness to heal. Briana took hers out. It took me several years more, but I eventually took mine out too.

You might be questioning why I just dropped such a large anecdote about a regrettable teenage piercing in the middle of this seemingly random list of facts about navels. You might be looking back to remember what omphaloskepsis is (see Navel-Gazer).

REGRET

Despite our teenage slogan, I do regret the piercing. Even all these years after I pierced it, I still find bits of lint not only in my actual belly button, but also in the incomplete scar from my stud.

I won't let my partner touch that either.

SEXY

For some, the belly button is an erogenous zone.

TELEVISION

In 1951, in a peculiar brand of omphalophobia (see Emit), "female navel exposure" was banned from US television because the exposed belly button was thought to be too powerful in inducing attraction.[20]

A decade later, Barbara Eden was prohibited from showing her navel on the famously Orientalist TV show *I Dream of Jeannie*.[21] Eden's pants had to cover her navel, or she had to wear fabric and skin-colored makeup to conceal it. It wasn't until 1985 that her costume became "low rise," revealing the navel.[22]

Exposure of "male navels" has rarely if ever been stigmatized like this.

The idea of "male" and "female" navels is ridiculous. Is it the navel's proximity to genitalia that has made it so controversial in western media? Or is it because of the literalness of the navel being another hole in a female body?

---

20. See Femina.
21. See Bergman and Archer.
22. See Hofstede.

UMBILICUS

Beneath the skin
            of the navel, clinically
                        known as
            the umbilicus,
a thick fibrous
            cord slithers.
                        This cord is
            a remnant
of the canal
            that drained
                        the bladder
            of the fetus
and ran within
            the umbilical cord.
                        Umbilical cord blood
            contains stem
cells like those
            in bone
                        marrow.

VISHNU

In Hinduism, the navel of Vishnu, the Preserver, is the center of the universe and the source of life.[23]

Before the universe is created, Vishnu sleeps on Shesha, the giant cobra—the serpent of infinity—who protects Vishnu and floats on the waters of a dark oceanic nothing. Vishnu sleeps peacefully. Then, from the inky depths, a resounding Om thrums the darkness with energy.

As morning dawns and Vishnu awakens, an elongated stalk emerges from his navel, revealing not a heart-shaped leaf (see Geography) but a lotus. From the center of the lotus, Brahma is revealed, hatched from an egg.

Brahma is the creator of this universe. He uses the petals of his lotus to make our world.

After 100 Brahma years, or roughly 3 trillion human years, Brahma attains liberation and pralaya, or massive floods, wash everything away.

Vishnu returns to his giant serpent bed to sleep and rest after all his years of caretaking. And then the cycle repeats again, and again.

In this creation story, from Vishnu's navel, an entire world is born and perishes and is born again. We again have the celebration of the navel as the center of birth and life and creativity. With the lotus, we also return to the enduring image of the navel as the connection of leaf and stem, and of the divine (see Geography; see Juncture).

In this story, however, the destruction of the world is inevitable, as is its rebirth. The cycles turn on and on.

Our dad, though he was born in India and to Hindu parents, wasn't raised with much to do with Hinduism. He converted to Christianity and assimilated to American life while growing up in segregated North Carolina in the 1950s and 60s.

Today, what I've learned about Hinduism and India is largely from books, the internet, and better-informed friends.

This severance is a kind of violence for us biracial diasporic daughters trying to unfurl our own brown roots and flower.

Even without knowing this story of Vishnu's navel, my sister Joya went through with a lotus birth[24] with her third child, who she and her husband named Omjabarindra, but who we call Omja or Om for short. Om was the first of her seven children to be born at home.

The lotus birth involves keeping the placenta and the umbilical cord intact after birth to dry and fall off on its own, a non-severance that honors the connection between placenta and baby, who some think of as being on the same energetic level, to let the baby's consciousness gently enter the body. The lotus birth honors the great transition of moving from the spirit world to the world incarnate, the world of being embodied.

"The placenta is like a grandmother," Joya said, "because it cared for the baby before it was in the mother's arms."

The natural drying and eventual dropping off of the umbilical cord allows for ongoing energy and cellular transfer to take place from the placenta to the baby.

Lotus birth protects the baby from their first wound, though the decomposing placenta and umbilical cord create their own challenges. Some rub the placenta and cord with salt and turmeric to aid the drying process.

It took seven days for Om's umbilical cord to wither and detach naturally.

"It smelled like the docks," Joya admitted. "But it was a nice gesture that we did."

Om, who is seventeen as of this writing, was also the baby Joya nursed longest.

"There's something to that," she said. "The lotus birth and his nursing. Om is a gentle boy. He still listens to me."

I wonder if, though Om's name came after he was born, the sound of what he would be called might have activated some ancestral knowing in Joya that told her a lotus should be born with him too.

Maybe that's a stretch.

Maybe not.

For her fourth, fifth, sixth, and seventh child, Joya did a partial lotus, which involves delaying severance of the umbilical cord for an hour or more after birth and is said to have similar benefits for the baby.

---

23. This retelling of this Hindu creation story stems from conversations with Dr. Rajiv Mohabir and references to Dimmitt and van Buitenen's text.

24. Midwife and author Jeannine Parvati Baker coined the terms "Lotus Birth" and "Free Birth" in the 1980s and 1990s. She influenced Joya's thinking about birth.

The navel

is the hub   or central part

of a wheel.

XENIAL

Given how many organisms live inside it, the navel is certainly xenial, or hospitable/friendly.

Also, finding words for the last few letters in abecedarian lists like this is virtually impossible to do without reaching for ridiculous, basically-never-used SAT words like xenial or, as you're about to see, yolk stalk.

YOLK STALK

The yolk stalk is a narrow tube that connects through the umbilical opening the early embryo to the yolk sac outside. The yolk stalk usually fades away, but a finger-like remnant might persist as a protrusion from the small intestine. Though very uncommon—this only occurs in 2 to 4 percent of people—this protrusion can become inflamed and require surgery to remove it.[25]

The yolk stalk is generally located in the lower right-hand side of the abdomen, about the same place my mom described her adhesion to be.

---

25. See Shiel.

Zzzzzz

Probably the worst critique to be launched against writers of creative nonfiction is that they are navel-gazers. The genre is populated by a bunch of narcissists who fling themselves on the outside world. What a snooze.

In her contribution to the anthology *The Far Edges of the Fourth Genre*, Kim Barnes states, "Readers of nonfiction should come away knowing more about themselves than they do about *you*." The emphasis, which appears in the original, might be a little hostile.

But how do readers learn about themselves by reading about someone else?

If writing creative nonfiction hones important writerly tools—self-reflection, meaning-making, attempts at understanding ourselves in relation to the worlds around us—reading creative nonfiction texts means observing the author's tools in practice.

At the risk of sounding defensive (and maybe a little hostile too), the appeal of reading this genre might be the unspoken invitation to experiment with the author's tools. So you can learn more about *yourself*.

Take this essay for example. You too can play an awkward game of finding odd facts about an enduring insult that gets you thinking about how your navel piercing was your own little adolescent act of individuating, or your mom's funny scar that has taken the place of her real belly button. And then you might learn about overlapping and diverging stories of creation, of leaves and stems, of long stalks and yolk stalks, and how full the world is of strange people and the things they make within it, including their very personal, very private, very disgusting navel products.

Why not try it?

See what you find in your metaphoric—or literal—navel. It might be body gunk. It might be the wound we need to heal. It might be a portal to the divine.

What's there will vary from person to person.

But, go on.

Take a look already.

NAVEL, NODAL, CURIOS
A CONVERSATION WITH ANJOLI ROY

Greetings, comrade! Thank you for talking to us about your process today! Can you introduce yourself, in a way that you would choose?

Sure thing! I am a creative writer and high school English teacher in Honolulu. I'm originally from Pasadena, California, which is Tongva land. My genre of choice is creative nonfiction. And, with my good friend Jocelyn Kapumealani Ng, I am also cohost of the literary and music podcast titled It's Lit (see itslitwithphdj.wordpress.com), which has featured more than 100 writers to date.

Why are you a "poet"/ "writer"/ "artist"?

We ask the folks we feature on our podcast a similar question, which is "Why lit?" and this happens to be my favorite question to ask, and yet I always stumble on how to answer it myself. I am a writer because stories shape our whole lives, and writing is the best way I am able to be attentive to this life. Writing makes me feel alive and present, and it allows me to try to make sense of the world around me. Writing things down is my attempt to preserve memories, which I nurse a fear of losing.

When did you decide to use the language you use for yourself (and/or: do you feel comfortable calling yourself a poet/writer/artist, what other titles or affiliations do you prefer/feel are more accurate)?

There are probably quite a lot of writers who struggle with imposter syndrome, and I certainly am one of them. There was a time when I thought I couldn't call myself a writer until I'd published a story. Then, when I'd done that, I decided I couldn't call myself a writer until I published a book. In short, the bar kept moving. At some point, I decided these thresholds were nonsense and remembered that, from a definitional standpoint, a writer is just a person who writes, so here I am today, telling folks I'm a writer.

What's a "poet" (or "writer" or "artist") anyway? What do you see as your cultural and social role (in the literary / artistic / creative community and beyond)?

Poets/writers/artists are those who have an impulse to create, and to create for an audience larger than themselves. There is a certain type of compulsion, perhaps, in imagining an audience beyond our journal pages and the loved ones we can foist our work upon.

As a writer and as a reader, I hope to produce the work I wished I had access to as a young person. I am mixed race (Bengali on my dad's side and German, English, Irish on my mom's), for example, and despite British colonial rule of the subcontinent, I grew up without access to mixed-race characters who looked like me and spoke to my experiences. The only Indian and white characters I encountered were white-passing children, written by authors who were not mixed themselves. The book-length project I drafted for my dissertation and which I am continuing to work on seeks to fill that gap.

So, in that sense, writing has been a selfish pursuit for me. But, I believe I'm not alone in this desire and seek out reading work about folks who do this same thing for themselves and their communities, even when their positionalities are quite different than mine. There's a power in taking back the narrative for ourselves, in writing ourselves into existence.

As we continue to speak for ourselves and read each other's varied voices, we become a more empathetic community. I believe in the transformative power of writing to facilitate this.

Talk about the process or instinct to move these poems (or your work in general) as independent entities into a body of work. How and why did this happen? Have you had this intention for a while? What encouraged and/or confounded this (or a book, in general) coming together? Was it a struggle?

I wrote this chapbook as a single work with the central conceit being an investigation into the epithet navel-gazing from a linguistic and personal perspective. I began with dictionary definitions from Oxford English Dictionary and decided to experiment with structuring the work on the alphabet, which I had a lot of fun with.

Writing is often a struggle. I have worked on personal stories that navigate ancestry and familial trauma. I have been the last person in the coffee shop, crying openly while shoveling a piece of gluten-free/dairy-free chocolate cake into my face, which I've tipped the barista for wildly on account of making things so awkward for the folks around me as I processed my shit, hopefully into art. But, writing this chapbook was joyous. I welcomed the process of discovery among the different threads that emerged as I wrote and I felt energized by the associations building upon each other as I continued to draft.

Did you envision this collection as a collection or understand your process as writing or making specifically around a theme while the poems themselves were being written / the work was being made? How or how not?

See above ☺

What formal structures or other constrictive practices (if any) do you use in the creation of your work? Have certain teachers or instructive environments, or

*readings/writings/work of other creative people informed the way you work/
write?*

In the summer 2019 issue of the literary magazine *Creative Nonfiction*, I
encountered the work of Julia Koets, whose titular story of her memoir
collection *The Rib Joint* plays with associative forms and odd facts about
octopus as she tells the story of falling in love with a person named Kate who
denies their love and demands it be kept secret for years. Koets's seeming use
of misdirection via the inclusion of anecdotes on how octopus escapes capture,
for example, acts as breather and curio amid the narrative arc of her (un?)love
story. As a reader, I found that this use of reprieves and interesting vistas into
the life of an octopus, if you will, worked really well on a metaphoric and, as
we learn toward the end of the story, a literal level (I won't say more on that, in
case you'd like to read the story too!).

Anyway, this essay inspired me to start experimenting with looser anecdotal
forms that felt more lyrical and invited the reader to complete the text's
meaning.

Robert Boswell, who teaches creative writing at the University of Texas, has
offered up the idea of authorial custody in writing, which is the extent to
which an author relinquishes control over the story after it has been put into
the hands of the reader. Lately, I have been thinking more about this concept
just as I teach it to my students.

Boswell says, "If the danger of a low-custody story is bewilderment of the
reader, the danger of a high-custody story is that it will be over-controlled,
telling the reader not only what happens but also how the reader should feel
about it. In such stories, the reader is passive and essentially redundant."

For my creative writing classes, I draw this idea on the white board. I chart
high custody as a dot high up on the board. High custody is where it is easy
to see and where less of the reader's imagination is at play. Then, I drawn an
arrow diagonally downward with an arrowhead at its base (who knows how
deep it goes). My class returns to this diagram throughout the semester as
we read progressively lower-custody work. Where does this story fall? I'll ask
them, and we'll debate where to chart it. As we enter the lyric, I draw a water
line and tell them that we are about to enter the rich and dark waters of loose
association. I tell them to brace themselves for potential bewilderment.

Stories like Koets's falls lower on the authorial custody spectrum and have
been useful inspiration for forms to experiment with, for me.

Of course, poets might role their eyes at this—many of them have been taking
the brave dive into the dark waters of low custody all along. I guess it's just
taken me a bit longer to work up the nerve.

Other authors who have influenced this form for me are Dinty W. Moore and his "Son of Mr. Green Jeans: A Meditation on Fathers," which, like this navel-gazing chapbook, is also an essay alphabetically arranged.

The authors who speak to my core/guts/navel(!) are those authors, many of whom are BIPOC and queer who write about ancestral connections and genealogies and who are doing the hard work to create community and heal, including Rajiv Mohabir, Noʻu Revilla, Aiko Yamashiro, Julia Katz, Jocelyn Kapumealani Ng, Bryan Kamaoli Kuwada, Lee Kava, Momi Cummings, Joseph Han, Will Giles, Malialina Derden, Terisa Siagatonu, Jahra Rager, Kathy Jetñil-Kijiner, Lyz Soto, D. Kealiʻi MacKenzie, Nicky Loomis, Craig Santos Perez, E.J. Koh, just to name a few writers who I love.

Speaking of monikers, what does your title represent? How was it generated? Talk about the way you titled the book, and how your process of naming (individual pieces, sections, etc) influences you and/or colors your work specifically.

I like the potential double meaning of this work's final primary title, which both demands that the reader physically travel into the navel, that potentially terrifying space for those with omphalophobia, and the secondary, perhaps more subtle reading, which is a stage direction where a navel might take bold strides onto a stage to perform for us.

The subtitle for this work, in light of the more poetic primary title, is a slightly higher-custody flourish, as I wanted the reader tipped off to the purpose of this chapbook before they began reading.

To be honest, this work has had more than one title. My original was "In Defense of Navel-Gazing: For the Love of Creative Nonfiction." This title worked for me, since the text is an apologia for the genre, just as it interrogates this epithet that is often launched at writers of creative nonfiction, but—in conjunction with the OS editors—we arrived at the current primary title, which is a bit more poetic.

What does this particular work represent to you as indicative of your method/ creative practice? your history? of your mission/intentions/hopes/plans?

This work marks a new departure for me in the kinds of writing I am currently pursuing. Since producing this navel story, I have drafted a few more chapbooks that are similar in their loose structures and exploratory natures, including:

- one on abalone and my grandfather, a waterman who was a skin diver and loved these mollusks the most, along with the histories of predation on abalone in the west coast of the US; I'm fascinated with this history and also how my grandfather, raised by a fisherman himself in New York's Long Island Sound, could have kids and grandkids who, unfortunately, hardly knew how to swim.

- a portrait on the house cat, beloved house pet and disease-addled foe, that addresses how cats domesticated themselves, their shifting place in western and eastern societies, and pieces of my own family history of living with a mom who loves cats and a dad who is terribly allergic to them (he once said he should have known their marriage was doomed when my mom started welcoming cats into the house).
- a linguistic dive into the definitions of the word "grind," which includes scientific information on bruxism, or chronic tooth grinding that most adults grow out of but unfortunately those in my family seem not to, along with suggestive slang connotations (as in "bump and ~").

This is all to say, where in the past I've been focused on writing toward the beautiful and to make sense of my and my families' histories, I have been taking on some more lighthearted writing via this form.

What does this book DO (as much as what it says or contains)?

At its core, I hope this chapbook convinces suspicious readers of the goodness in creative nonfiction's alleged navel-gazing.

What would be the best possible outcome for this book? What might it do in the world, and how will its presence as an object facilitate your creative role in your community and beyond? What are your hopes for this book, and for your practice?

As the ending of this chapbook states, I hope readers go down similar rabbit holes that might bring them to a greater sense of curiosity about the world around us just as they learn more about themselves. We are more agile and careful humans, the more we know about our own histories and the histories of the places that we have been calling home. I hope this chapbook demonstrates some of the fruits that can come from this exercise.

Personally, having this chapbook in the world as an object helps me feel more capital-W writerly, to go back to your earlier question about how and when I started calling myself a writer. Thank you, OS team!

What does it mean to make books in this time, and what are your thoughts around shifting into digital books/objects and digital access in general?

I was thinking recently about how I am a breed of reader who likes to have hard copies in my hands to mark up and make notes across physical pages (this is how I remember stories best), but I'm also someone who wishes they had a keyword-search function in print books. Integrated technology that does this doesn't exist yet, but maybe the middle ground is having books available both in print to purchase and in free digital formats to peruse online.

Overall, I think that it's wonderful to make books available to all online and for free. I do wonder a bit about how this free distribution might work for publishers and authors who put the work in to create this content, though. The folks at OS work for free, which is part of why this free model works, but I also feel that excellent editorial work deserves compensation. Also, authors deserve compensation for their hard-won work, particularly since we still live in a world with reading fees, which drive dollars out of authors' pockets. What would equitable publishing truly look like? I wonder.

All this said, I'm grateful to have this weird little chapbook out in the world gratis and that it also can be a physical object to hold in your hands, if you decide to purchase it. I'm grateful it will be available in both forms.

Let's talk a little bit about the role of poetics and creative community in social and political activism, so present in our daily lives as we face the often sobering, sometimes dangerous realities of the Capitalocene. The publication of these volumes now falls during an ongoing global pandemic, intersecting with the largest collective uprising in US history, with Black Lives Matter, dismantling white supremacy, and abolition at the fore. How does your process, practice, or work reflect these conditions?

This is a big and vital question. The work that I am drawn to as a reader and that I hope to speak to as an author is able to engage these difficult questions of our current revolutionary moments in meaningful ways. One of the many assets of the creative arts is the ability to engage feeling directly in the pursuit of greater truths. That said, I find myself often as someone who is so caught up in feeling during moments like this pandemic, this crucial uprising for Black lives, and the calls for each and every one of us to do the work to dismantle white supremacy, including abolishing the police and prisons, that I find myself struggling to find words. I think this, in part, is the reason I started up with podcasting.

Jocelyn and I have been putting out themed calls for materials (for the water protectors at Standing Rock, for an end to further desecration of Maunakea, for responses to the COVID-19 pandemic, for the current BLM Uprising) since the inception of It's Lit back in 2016.

I feel indebted to those writers who we have featured who are moved to write quickly, potently, and thoroughly, helping us listeners put words to our feelings and act.

A strong literary process, practice, and work are fed directly by this.

I'd be curious to hear some of your thoughts on the challenges we face in speaking and publishing across lines of race, age, ability, class, privilege, social/cultural background, gender, sexuality (and other identifiers) within the community as well as creating and maintaining safe spaces, vs. the dangers of remaining and producing in isolated "silos" and/or disciplinary and/or institutional bounds?

The more we know our own stories, the better we can engage with each other's. I cannot write about my story without engaging race, age, ability, class, privilege, social/cultural background, gender, sexuality, and more. If we bring light to our own markers, the more thoughtful and careful we will likely be in regards to our differences.

For example, I am a writer in a brown body who cannot escape that brownness, even if I wanted to (which I do not). That awareness informs how I read the ways other writers talk about their experiences of their racialized bodies, their gender identities, the words they use to talk about who they love and how they describe their sexuality, for example. Learning more about my family history teaches me how to listen when others share their stories. It teaches me, as a resident who loves this nation, the importance of learning about, putting my weight behind, and being sure to include in my curricula Hawai'i's fight for sovereignty.

This work is how safe spaces are fought and won, and it is how we resist silos in order to speak with, listen to, and care for each other.

REFERENCES

American Museum of Natural History. "Microbiome Monday: The Ecosystem in Your Belly Button." *AMNH.org*, 25 Sept. 2015, https://www. amnh.org/explore/news-blogs/news-posts/microbiome-monday-the-ecosystem-in-your-belly-button. Accessed 4 June 2020.

Barnes, Kim. "The Art and Absence of Reflection in Personal Nonfiction: What Is the Why?" *The Far Edges of the Fourth Genre*, edited by Sean Prentiss and Joe Wilkins, Michigan State University Press, 2014, pp. 133– 41.

"Belly Button Biodiversity." *National Geographic*, 22 May 2013, https://www. nationalgeographic.org/article/belly-button-biodiversity/. Accessed 22 Nov. 2019.

Bergman, Gregory, and Peter Archer. *I Watch, Therefore I Am: From Socrates to Sartre, the Great Mysteries of Life as Explained Through Howdy Doody, Marcia Brady, Homer Simpson, Don Draper, and Other TV Icons*. Adams Media, 2011.

Boswell, Robert. "Having Gravity and Having Weight: On Meaning in Fiction." 2013, https://www.graywolfpress.org/robert-boswell-having-gravity-and-having-weight. Accessed 1 Dec. 2019.

Bright Side. "18 Reasons Your Belly Button Is a Very Intriguing Body Part." *YouTube*, 24 Feb. 2018, https://www.youtube.com/watch?v=1a5_cAWVveY. Accessed 21 Nov. 2019.

Capetta, Amy. "How Normal Is Your Navel? Belly Button Facts and Figures You Probably Didn't Know." *Everyday Health*, 21 Apr. 2011, https://www. everydayhealth.com/healthy-living/0421/how-normal-is-your-belly-button.aspx. Accessed 4 June 2020.

Daily Mail Reporter. "Librarian Enters the Guiness Book of Records for Collecting 22.1 Grams of 'Belly Button Fluff' over 26 Years." *Dailymail. co.uk*, 25 Oct. 2010, https://www.dailymail.co.uk/news/article-1323477/ Record-breaking-belly-fluff-collection-Graham-Barker-collected-22-1g-26-years.html. Accessed 4 June 2020.

Dell'Amore, Christine. "Women Can Make New Eggs after All, Stem-Cell Study Hints." *National Geographic News*, 1 Mar. 2012, https://www. nationalgeographic.com/news/2012/3/120229-women-health-ovaries-eggs-reproduction-science/. Accessed 28 Nov. 2019.

Dimmitt, Cornelia, and J.A.B. van Buitenen. *Classical Hindu Mythology: A Reader in the Sanskrit Puranas*. Temple University Press, 1978.

Femina, Jerry Della. *From Those Wonderful Folks Who Gave You Pearl Harbor: Front-Line Dispatches from the Advertising War*. Canongate Books, 2010.

Fischer, Shannon. "What Lives in Your Belly Button? Study Finds 'Rain Forest' of Species." *National Geographic*, 4 Nov. 2012, https://www.

nationalgeographic.com/news/2012/11/121114-belly-button-bacteria-science-health-dunn/#close. Accessed 4 June 2020.

Henderson, Corey, and Dan Rollman. *The Recordsetter Book of World Records*. Workman Publishing, 2011.

Hofstede, David. *What Were They Thinking? The 100 Dumbest Events in Television History*. Back Stage Books, 2004.

Hulcr, Jiri, Andrew M. Latimer, Jessica B. Henley, Nina R. Rountree, Noah Fierer, Andrea Lucky, Margaret D. Lowman, and Robert R. Dunn. "A Jungle in There: Bacteria in Belly Buttons Are Highly Diverse, but Predictable." 7 Nov. 2012, *PLoS ONE* vol. 7, no. 11, p. e47712, https://doi.org/10.1371/journal.pone.0047712. Accessed 4 June 2020.

Illinois Department of Public Health. "Facts about Postpartum Depression." N.d., http://www.idph.state.il.us/about/womenshealth/factsheets/pdpress. htm. Accessed 24 Nov. 2019.

Kim, Gene, and Benji Jones. "A Biologist Once Made Cheese with Belly-Button Bacteria. Here's How That's Possible." 10 Jul. 2019, https://www. businessinsider.com/belly-button-innie-inside-cheese-bacteria-lint-fungi-2019-7. Accessed 3 Dec. 2019.

Koets, Julia. "The Rib Joint." *Creative Nonfiction*, summer 2019, issue 71, pp. 63–71.

Kuwada, Bryan Kamaoli. "We Live in the Future. Come Join Us." *Ke Kaʻupu Hehi ʻAle*, 3 Apr. 2015, https://hehiale.wordpress.com/2015/04/03/we-live-in-the-future-come-join-us/. Accessed 1 Dec. 2019

MacKenzie, Macaela. "Why Belly Button Plastic Surgery Procedures Are Trending Right Now." *Allure*, 16 Feb. 2018, https://www.allure.com/story/belly-button-plastic-surgery-procedures. Accessed 4 June 2020.

Maly, Kepa, and Onaona Maly. "Mauna Kea—Ka Piko Kaulana O Ka ʻĀina: A Collection of Native Traditions, Historical Accounts, and Oral History Interviews for Mauna Kea, the Lands of Kaʻohe, Humuʻula and the ʻĀina Mauna on the Island of Hawaiʻi." *Ulukau*, 30 March 2005, http://www. ulukau.org/elib/cgi-bin/library?e=d-0mauna-000Sec--11haw-50-20-frameset-book--1-010escapewin&a=d&d=D0&toc=0

"Manipura Chakra: Navel Center." *Chakras.net*. N.d., https://www.chakras. net/energy-centers/manipura/about-the-manipura-chakra. Accessed 4 June 2020.

Muramoto, Hiroyoki. "Celebrating the Navel in Japan's 'Belly Button.'" *Reuters Lifestyle*, 27 July 2008, https://www.reuters.com/article/us-japan-bellybutton/celebrating-the-navel-in-japans-belly-button-idUSSP29709920080728. Accessed 4 June 2020.

"Navel." *Encyclopaedia Britannica*. 19 June 2020, https://www.britannica. com/science/navel. Accessed 24 July 2020.

"Navel." *Oxford English Dictionary*. Accessed 1 Dec. 2019.

"Omphaloskepsis." *Merriam-Webster*. N.d., https://www.merriam-webster. com/dictionary/omphaloskepsis. Accessed 1 Dec. 2019.

"Piko." *Nā Puke Wehewehe ʻŌlelo Hawaiʻi*. N.d., http://wehewehe.org/ gsdl2.85/cgi-bin/hdict?a=q&r=1&hs=1&m=-1&o=-1&qto=4&e=p-11000-00---off-0hdict--00-1----0-10-0---0---0direct-10-ED--4--textpukuielbert%252ctextmamaka-----0-1l--11-haw-Zz-1---Zz-1-home--00-3-1-00-0--4----0-0-11-00-0utfZz-8-00&q=piko&fqv=textpukuielbert

%252ctextmamaka&af=1&fqf=ED. Accessed 1 Dec. 2019.

The Public Science Lab. "Belly Button Biodiversity." North Carolina State University, Department of Applied Ecology, n.d., http://robdunnlab.com/projects/belly-button-biodiversity/. Accessed 3 June 2020.

———. "Common Belly Button Bacteria." North Carolina State University, Department of Applied Ecology, n.d., http://robdunnlab.com/projects/belly-button-biodiversity/most-common/. Accessed 3 June 2020.

Roy, Anjoli. "Grandpa Was a Skin Diver: 20 Directives for a Wet-Cat Granddaughter." *Anomaly*, forthcoming.

———. "Little Red BMW." *StoryQuarterly*, no. 52, 2019, pp. 203–216.

———. "What Babas Are For." *ExPatLit.com: A Literary Review for Writers Abroad*, 2010.

Sabrina. "Ripley's Strangest Collection: Unboxing Belly Button Lint." *Ripleys.com*, 20 May 2018, https://www.ripleys.com/weird-news/strangest-collection/. Accessed 4 June 2020.

Satyres In Atlante. Louvre. N.d., http://cartelfr.louvre.fr/cartelfr/visite?srv=car_not_frame&idNotice=9495. Accessed 4 June 2020.

Shiel, William C. "Medical Definition of Yolk Stalk." *Medicine Net*, n.d., https://www.medicinenet.com/script/main/art.asp?articlekey=6064. Accessed 22 Nov. 2019.

UNILAD. "Guy Has 'Biggest Outie Belly Button in the World.'" 28 March 2018, https://www.unilad.co.uk/featured/guy-with-one-inch-long-belly-button-reveals-weirdest-request-hes-had/. Accessed 24 Nov 2019.

ACKNOWLEDGMENTS

I have a lot of thank-yous to folks for helping me with this weird little chapbook.

First off, thank you to Orchid Tierney and Curtis Emery at the OS for accepting this work for publication, and for doing so within a month of when I submitted it for their consideration. What a thrill! Thank you to Elæ [Lynne DeSilva-Johnson] for the cover design, and thank you, Orchid, for your careful typesetting.

Huge thank-yous to my dear friends Rajiv Mohabir and Bryan Kamaoli Kuwada for their help, expertise, and feedback on the entries on Hindu and Hawaiian creation stories included in these pages, respectively.

Rajiv, thank you for the section about Vishnu, and for your tireless feedback on and unflagging support of my writing in general. Your hands are on this text, whether you like touching navels or not(!). But, really, any interesting line breaks or poetic formats are yours, obviously. Thank you, star. I am unworthy of your light. Come home already.

Bryan, I appreciate your guidance with the sections about Maunakea and Hāloa in particular and for teasing me basically all the time about all the things I'm self-conscious about, including how to talk about how much Hawaiʻi continues to teach me. A cat is ever squirmy and grateful for your generosity of spirit and breadth of knowledge and your reassuring friendship.

I owe my tendency to go down rabbit holes for odd phrases, family histories, and ancestral knowledges to graduate work at the University of Hawaiʻi at Mānoa and my work at the Center for Biographical Research especially. Thank you to Cynthia G. Franklin, Craig Howes, Caroline Sinavaiana, and John Zuern for challenging and opening up my brain to the complexity of telling true stories. Thank you to Elizabeth Colwill for the gentle nudge to write. Thank you to my caring and supportive dissertation chair, S. Shankar (I hope this little book makes you laugh!). Thank you to Shawna Yang Ryan, who encouraged me and said modular, linked forms were something I ought seriously to consider playing with. Thank you to Craig Santos Perez, who in his Pacific Poetry and Poetics course offered up the helpful idea of what it might mean to be like tea here in Hawaiʻi, and to Allison Adelle Hedge Coke for her ongoing support.

Thank you for my dear ones here in Hawaiʻi and overseas who continue to nurture creativity and challenge and inspire and give me life in all kinds of ways. Your names ought to be on any work I manage to put out into the world: Aiko Yamashiro, Noʻu Revilla, Luseane Raass, CJ Kee, Jocelyn Kapumealani Ng, Lei Bong, Julia Katz, Momi Cummings, Joy Enomoto, Kim Compoc, Lee Kava, Joseph Han, Dax Garcia, Marion Cadora, Elise Leimomi Dela Cruz-Talbert, Jessica Maust Dahle (bff4lyfe!), Nicky Loomis, Aisha Wagner, Samali Lubega, Briana Headman, (the octogenarian woman we will one day be), Michelle Hirst, B.J. De Guzman, Nicolet Gatewood, Devi Laskar who we call Ritun, my VONA fam, including Bich Minh Nguyen, and and and! There are more dear ones in my heart than names I can fit on a page. I love and am grateful to every one of you.

For permission to tell these navel-gazing stories on each one of us, thank you to piercing-partner Briana and my family, including especially my third nephew, Omja; my sisters, Joya and Maya; and our parental units, Subi and Dotti. Not everybody has a family who will read their strange stories and say they like them, even when they reveal us. I'm so fortunate to have been born into ours. Is there a portal to come be with you yet?? The Pacific Ocean has never been so big than in these pandemic times. I love and miss you so much.

Last and certainly not least, deep thanks to my partner, Eldridge Shay, who listened to me read aloud drafts one through ninety-seven (not really, but close) of this chapbook. He almost never fell asleep in the process and has been, without fail, encouraging and supportive of me, even when I leave all the lights on in our little studio and laugh at dictionary entries and YouTube videos about belly buttons late into the night. Thank you, love, for being interested in the odd stories that shift around in my head and for seeing me so clearly. I am so lucky to love with you.

ABOUT THE AUTHOR

ANJOLI ROY studied English and creative writing at the University of Hawaiʻi at Mānoa, where she earned a PhD. A VONA fellow and a Pushcart and Best of the Net nominee, Anjoli is a mashi to eight, a godmother to one, and the last of her parents's three girls. You can find her online at www.anjoliroy.com and on Twitter and Facebook @anjoliroy. She'd love to hear from you...

WHY PRINT:DOCUMENT?
(AND WHAT DOES THIS MEAN FOR DIGITAL MEDIA?)

The Operating System has traditionally used the language "print:document" to differentiate from the book-object as part of our mission to distinguish the act of documentation-in-book-FORM from the act of publishing as a backwards-facing replication of the book's agentive *role* as it may have appeared the last several centuries of its history. Ultimately, we approach the book as TECHNOLOGY: one of a variety of documents across a range of media that humans have invented and in turn used to archive and disseminate ideas, beliefs, stories, and other evidence of production.

Ownership and use of printing presses and access to (or restriction of) information/materials, libraries, and archives has long been a site of struggle, related in many ways to revolutionary activity and the fight for civil rights and free speech all over the world. While (in many countries) the contemporary quotidian landscape has indeed drastically shifted in its access to platforms for sharing information and in the widespread ability to "publish" digitally, even with extremely limited resources, the importance of publication on physical media has not diminished. In fact, this may be the most critical time in recent history for activist groups, artists, and others to insist upon learning, establishing, and encouraging personal and community documentation practices.

With The OS's print endeavors I wanted to open up a conversation about this: the ultimately radical, transgressive act of creating PRINT / DOCUMENTATION in the digital age. It's a question of the archive, and of history: who gets to tell the story, and what evidence of our lives, our behaviors, and/or our experiences are we leaving behind? We can know little to nothing about the future into which we're leaving an unprecedentedly digital document trail--but we can be assured that publications, government agencies, museums, schools, and other institutional powers that be will continue to leave BOTH a digital and print version of their production for the official record. Will we?

As a (rogue) anthropologist and long time academic, I can easily pull up many accounts about how lives, behaviors, experiences--how THE STORY of a time or place--was pieced together using the deep study of the archive: correspondence, notebooks, and other physical documents which are no longer the norm in many lives and practices. As we move our creative behaviors towards digital note taking, and even audio and video, what can we predict about future technology that is in any way assuring that our stories will be accurately told--or told at all? How will we leave these things for the record?

For all our years of print publication, I've said that "with these documents we say: WE WERE HERE, WE EXISTED, WE HAVE A DIFFERENT STORY", but now, with the rapid expansion of greater volume with digital and DIY printed media, we add: we ARE here, and while we are, we will not be limited in what we add value to, share, make accessible, or give voice to, by restricting it to what we can afford to print in volume.

Adding a digital series is the next chapter of *our* story: a way for us to support more creative practitioners and offer folks independent options for POD or DIY-zine-style distribution, even without our financial means changing -- which means, each book will *also* have archive-ready print manifestations. It's our way of challenging what is required to evolve and grow. Ever onward, outward, beyond.

Elæ [Lynne DeSilva-Johnson]. Founder& Creative Director
THE OPERATING SYSTEM, Brooklyn NY 2019

BLOOM, MUTATION, ENTROPY, CATALYST, BRINE

In the fall of 2019, we posted the following call for digital chapbooks through our variegated Operating System networks:

> How queer is climate change? What mutating futurities are possible in writings of the diaspora? How do we imagine evolving micro/macro/plant-based/insect-like scales of environmental disturbance? How salty is survival? What kind of archive is the ocean? What will become of history under water? We invite writers to submit works that speak to our ecological moment, apprehend change, reaction, and action in networked and local ways, and explore the multiple and the contingent.

This call for submissions centred around the metaphoric, the contingent, the liminal, and the fluvial. But most of all, it drew its strengths from the desire of and for the language of persistence. With so much at stake in the current motions of precarity—climate change, rising sea levels, ecological degradation, racial injustice, police brutality, and now the global COVID-19 pandemic—we wondered: how can we serve as decentred world citizens and retain the critical thrust of the archival through networks over nodal institutions and Big Poetry? What duties of care does form have to shared histories and collective memories? What nuances of language must we co-develop to imagine humane infrastructures?

The call for submissions drew many submissions that approached and reimagined the document as dispersive and fluvial. They were all radically beautiful and critically-engaging. Ultimately, we selected six manuscripts, which we felt reflected a momentary grappling for the micro-macro that forced us as coordinators to reimagine the frayed edges of our call.

The Operating System is committed to fostering open-resource and share-alike cultures for mutual aid, direct support, and radical organising. In the spirit of the wet archive, we encourage you to share, digitally store, print, and support authors via our Open Access library.

Curtis Emery and Orchid Tierney
Digital Chapbook Coordinators 2020

THE 2020 OS CHAPBOOK SERIES

DIGITAL TITLES:

Recall - Lee Gough

The Woman Factory - Ava Hofmann

Kind Haven - Jacob Kobina Ayiah Mensah

Lichen Land - J Pascutazz

Enter The Navel: For The Love Of Creative Nonfiction -Anjoli Roy

Witch Like Me - Sunnylyn Thibodeaux

***

PLEASE SEE OUR FULL CATALOG
FOR FULL LENGTH VOLUMES AND PREVIOUS CHAPBOOK SERIES:
HTTP://WWW.THEOPERATINGSYSTEM.ORG/

DOC U MENT
/däkyəmənt/

First meant "instruction" or "evidence," whether written or not.

Who is responsible for the manufacture of value?

Based on what supercilious ontology have we landed in a space where we vie
against other creative people in vain pursuit of the fleeting credibilities
of the scarcity economy, rather than freely collaborating and sharing
openly with each other in ecstatic celebration of MAKING?

While we understand and acknowledge the economic pressures and fear-mongering
that threatens to dominate and crush the creative impulse, we also believe
that now more than ever we have the tools to relinquish agency
via cooperative means, fueled by the fires of the Open Source Movement.

Looking out across the invisible vistas of that rhizomatic parallel country
we can begin to see our community beyond constraints, in the place
where intention meets resilient, proactive, collaborative organization.

Here is a document born of that belief, sown purely of imagination and will.
When we document we assert. We print to make real, to reify our being there.
When we do so with mindful intention to address our process,
to open our work to others, to create beauty in words in space,
to respect and acknowledge the strength of the page we now hold
physical, a thing in our hand… we remind ourselves that,
like Dorothy: we had the power all along, my dears.

the PRINT! DOCUMENT SERIES

is a project of
the trouble with bartleby
in collaboration with
the operating system